Monty

THE BEST DOG EVER!

Barbara Norwood

authorHOUSE®

AuthorHouse™
1663 Liberty Drive
Bloomington, IN 47403
www.authorhouse.com
Phone: 1 (800) 839-8640

Published by AuthorHouse 12/04/2015

ISBN: 978-1-5049-3322-3 (sc)
ISBN: 978-1-5049-3321-6 (e)

Library of Congress Control Number: 2015913759

Print information available on the last page.

Contents

Introduction

This book has been written to acknowledge the fact that all of us can and do love our pets that we have living in our homes with us as a family member.

When our pets die we grieve. We feel real sorrow and loss. Sometimes we are so heart- broken that we cannot even speak but we continue to cry by ourselves and feel foolish for crying over a pet.

The love of a pet is as real as the love we feel for each other or very close to that same degree.

Let us not be ashamed to cry and show our broken hearts over the loss of our pets. God made all animals for man to love and the Bible clearly states that fact. Just know that all pets go to Heaven after they die because God created them and thought of all animals as very special.

Dedication

This book is dedicated to my children Bridget, Angela and Ernest and to my brothers and sisters who supported my dream and gave me hope that I might someday write a book or even two.

I would like to also thank my sister Jeannette for bringing Monty home to our mother who is Gramma Blair in this story.

Thank you to Paula my sister-in-law and my daughters Bridget and Angela and my great-granddaughter Aubrie for reading my first attempt at this book and for advising that I make a few corrections.

Monty The Best Dog Ever

This is a true story of a bonding love that developed between a family and a dog named Monty.

Story by: Barbara Norwood

Illustrations by: Barbara Norwood

Aubrie P. Duval

Tribute to Monty

Written by: Sara K. Norwood

Monty Lives With Gramma Blair

Monty lived in a big house with an older lady named Gramma Blair. Monty was a puppy.

Monty loved to jump and run very fast! Gramma Blair
could not jump or run with Monty.

Gramma Blair had a grandson named Ernie who really loved Monty and played with Monty every time he visited Gramma Blair.

Gramma Blair knew her grandson Ernie loved Monty as much as she did. Gramma Blair knew Ernie would take good care of Monty and give him lots of love and a good home. Gramma Blair asked Ernie if he would like to keep Monty as his own pet.

Ernie said he would take Monty home that day. Gramma Blair told Ernie that he could have Monty only if he promised never to give him away to anyone else. If Ernie could not keep the dog than he was to bring Monty back to Gramma Blair.

Ernie Takes Monty Home

Ernie took Monty home to meet his new family. Ernie had a white cat named Alby. Ernie's mom and dad had a small dog and his name was Skippy.

Ernie ran and jumped with his new friend Monty! Monty learned new tricks and followed Ernie wherever he went. Monty loved his new family and protected everyone that lived in his new home.

Ernie would brush Monty's hair until it shined. In the spring Monty's hair would fall out to keep his body cool in the warm weather. In the winter Monty's hair would grow back in to keep his body warm in the cold weather.

Ernie made sure Monty ate all the right foods and exercised every day. Monty's body became very strong.

Ernie wanted Monty to feel special so he always kept a loose, clean, red scarf around Monty's neck. Monty felt special when he wore the red scarf so he would strut around the driveway.

Sometimes Ernie would have to take Monty to the Veterinarian who is an animal doctor. Monty needed to have his teeth checked and had to have a few shots and flea medication to help his body stay healthy.

When we buy or have an animal given to us we need to take good care of that animal. Monty knew Ernie loved him, fed him and kept him healthy and safe.

One day Ernie's cat Alby was playing outside near the brook when a large snake decided to bully Alby. Monty saw the snake bothering him so he jumped across the brook and saved Alby from the snake.

One summer afternoon Monty was laying on the garage floor watching Ernie fix his red truck. Outside the garage door Skippy was laying in the driveway enjoying the warmth of the Sun.

All of a sudden Monty jumped up in a flash, gave a bark and a deep growl as he leaped up into the air and landed right in front of the sleeping Skippy and stood facing another big dog who was just about to hurt Skippy. Monty chased the big dog away and saved little Skippy. Monty was a hero!

Sometimes Monty would even cry because he was sad that someone in his family was sick. Dogs can learn to take care of people and love them back if we treat them as part of the family.

After high school graduation Ernie went on to attend college but Ernie still took Monty for rides in his car, played Frisbee, ball and taught Monty how to do hi-5 with his paws.

If Ernie would be coming home late from college or work he would ask his parents to take care of Monty until he came home. When we have a pet living in our home we must make sure the pet will be taken care of by someone else when we are not able to take care of them ourselves.

Monty Meets Ernie's New Friend

Ernie met a lady named Sara. Ernie introduced Sara to his dog Monty.

Sara was not sure if she liked Monty.

Monty was a big dog with big teeth!

After a few days went by Monty knew that he liked Sara.
He followed her all over the yard and wanted to go with
her when she went to the grocery store.

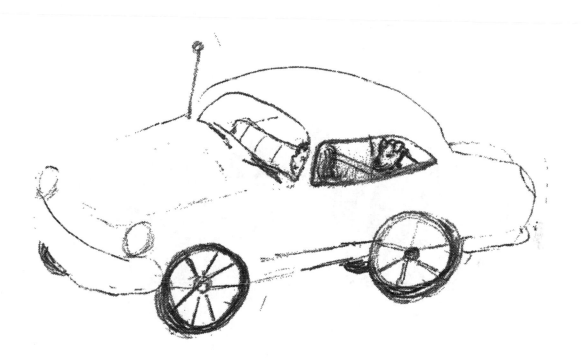

Sara decided that she liked Monty too! Monty was allowed to hop into the back seat of Sara's new car to ride to the store.

Monty waited in the car while Sara did her shopping. When Sara came back to the car she was holding a paper bag filled with good things to eat. Sara sat the paper bag on the back seat right next to Monty!

Monty would have liked to have eaten the goodies in the bag but he knew that would not be the right thing to do. Monty was a very smart dog. Monty knew if he was a good boy he would be allowed to go with Sara again.

Monty Joins Ernie and Sara

Ernie asked Sara to marry him and Sara said yes. Monty now would live with Ernie and Sara in their new home. Monty would be the first one to be part of their new life together as a family.

Monty loved being with Ernie no matter where he went
or lived. Monty protected Sara and Ernie and their new
home. Monty protected them because he loved them and
knew they loved and protected him, too.

Sometimes Sara would put a hat on Monty. Monty would wear sunglasses too. Monty was a fun dog. He loved attention and praise. Monty loved being a part of the family.

Monty Moves To Colorado

One day Sara began to pack Monty's toys, blanket and his food dishes. Monty was moving to Colorado with Sara and Ernie. Monty was a very good dog and was loved very much and was a big part of this family so he would travel with Ernie and Sara to their new home. When we treat our animals as part of our family they begin to love us as much as we love them.

Monty was a bit nervous about watching his food dishes and toys being packed but once he was in the car and on his way to Colorado he decided to take a nap. Monty only had one accident but people also make mistakes and accidents sometimes happen when they are excited or do not understand what is happening. Even dogs need time to learn how to be patient.

Monty had lots of room to play in his new yard! He chased butterflies, squirrels and Frisbees. Monty ran fast and made funny noises as he tried to communicate with Ernie

Everyone needs a friend. Even dogs need another dog or cat to play with during the day while their family members are at work or in school.

Monty was lonely in Colorado without his old friends back in New Hampshire so Sara decided that Monty needed a new friend. Sara went to the animal shelter and found a new friend for Monty.

When we give our animals love they learn to love, too. Monty decides to like and take care of the new dog. The new dog's name will be Bella.

Monty was happy to have a friend but he was not sure if
he really wanted to share his toys or the people he loved
with his new friend Bella.

Monty Welcomes Samuel

One day Sara and Ernie came home with a small baby boy named Samuel. Monty and Bella seemed to be very excited about the new baby. Sara and Ernie needed to teach Monty and Bella how to behave around the new baby.

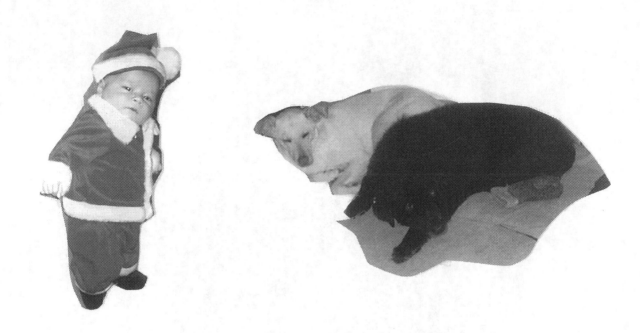

When we decide to add or bring a new member into our family we have to teach our animals how to live with the new member. First we introduce the new member to the old members of the family. Next, we have to set up some rules so that each of the members in the family are safe and happy.

Monty loves Ernie and Sara and he knows that they love him too; so Monty will take good care of their baby and his new friend Bella. Monty is a happy dog because he has been made a big part of his family.

Ernie and Sara's friends loved Monty too! Some of their friends tried to find a dog just like Monty but they could not find one. If you want a dog like Monty, you need to teach your dog to behave and reward the dog when he does a good job with love, a pat on the head and maybe a treat.

Monty Moves To Indiana

Ernie has a new job in Indiana so the family will be moving in a few weeks. Monty sees Sara packing his food dish and toys along with Bella's and Samuel's.

Monty knows what is going to happen this time and he will be ready for the move. Bella and Samuel are unsure of what is happening so Monty will comfort both of them.

Monty likes his new home in Indiana. The house is much bigger and he has more room to run and play outside with Bella and Sam.

As Samuel grows bigger Monty tries to play with him as much as possible. Monty watches television with Samuel and Bella. Samuel uses Monty for a pillow. Monty's hair is so soft.

Monty does not eat as much as he did before. He does not want to play or run everyday either. Monty does not hear and his eyes do not see the ball as quickly as they use to. Monty likes to sleep most of the day now.

Monty has lived for fifteen years and now he has become very tired. Sara and Ernie will bring Monty to the Veterinarian for a check up. Fifteen years of age in a dog's life would be 105 years in a human's life. Monty has lived a long life.

The Veterinarian said that Monty was just very old and it was time for him to rest. Monty was a good dog and took care of his family and friends but he was tired now.

Monty passed away and his family cried. They miss him very much and that's okay because Monty was a part of their family too. Monty made them laugh and kept them safe with his love. Monty was a special dog with a special master and a very special family.

Monty was the best dog ever!

After Monty passed away Ernie and Sara brought home another new baby named Rebecca. Monty had shown Bella how to love and protect the family so now Bella will take care of Samuel and Rebecca.

Testimony-Monty Goes To Heaven

After Monty passed away his family was very sad and they cried. Monty was a big part of their lives. He made them laugh and kept them all safe. The family posted a tribute to Monty over the internet.

The tribute has been added to this book in remembrance of Monty.

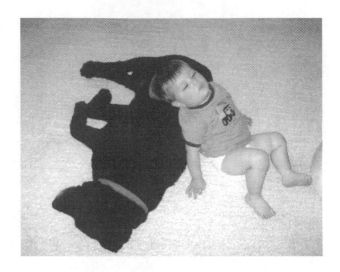

You loved kids, and your ears would perk up whenever you heard them playing outside.

You were always gentle with Samuel, even when he would pet you a little too enthusiastically, or would claim your blanket as his own.

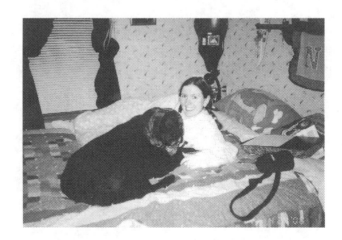

You didn't jump up on people or lick them. In fact, you so rarely gave kisses that it was an honor to get one from you. You loved for people to pat you, and if they stopped, you would nudge their hand with your head for more.

With the exception of the evil squirrel that taunted you and Bella in Parker, you were always nice to other animals.

You had a wonderful fashion sense, and loved to show that off.

You were Ernie's faithful companion since he was 19 years old. You two loved to go for walks in the woods in New Hampshire and for rides in Ernie's truck.

We were blessed to have you in our family for as long as we did.

Although we are sad you are no longer here, we know you are in a better place now. A place where you can walk without pain, a place where there are no scary thunderstorms or fireworks. A place where perhaps, a giant conveyor belt goes past all day long bringing you bowls of ice cream, pieces of bacon, and your favorite cheez-its.

We love you Monty, and we always will.

How To Have A Monty Dog

Instructions on how to have a Monty Dog:

1. When you bring a new dog into your home and family take time to get to know your new dog.

2. Give your new dog time to get to know and trust you.

3. Protect your dog from harm.

4. Introduce your new dog to the rest of your family.

5. Be sure your dog has a bed to sleep in (or his/her own area) and make sure your dog knows that this space belongs to him/her.

6. Make sure your dog has his/her own toys, balls and maybe a special blanket to play tug of war with. Dogs love attention and play time.

7. Check often for ticks, fleas and cuts on your dog's body and feet.

8. Brush your dog's hair often.

9. Try to walk your dog at least once a day.

10. Do not leave your dog outside in the rain or cold winter months for long periods at a time especially without shelter.

11. Have your Veterinarian show you how to clean your dog's ears and eyes and how to brush the dog's teeth.

12. Talk softly to your dog when you are inspecting his/her ears, eyes and teeth. The dog will start to understand what you are doing and saying if you make this a routine.

13. Be sure your dog has plenty of fresh water to drink everyday.

14. Ask your veterinarian what kind of food would be best to feed your dog.

15. Give your dog a bath when needed.

16. Play with your dog and teach him/her new tricks. Reward the dog with a treat when he/she learns a new trick.

17. Teach your dog new commands such as "sit down," "catch," "no," "go," "stop," "shake hands," and any other words that you would like your dog to learn.

18. Ask your dog to come to you when he/she has to go out or needs help for some other reason.

19. When you go on vacation have someone you can trust take care of your dog while you are away. If possible take your dog with you on vacation.

20. Our pets should be taught by us to get along with other animals that they will encounter each day.

21. Animals need to have a physical checkup once a year just as people do. Take your pet to the Veterinarian for examinations and medications to protect them against ticks and fleas.

22. Make sure you always have an adult present as you help with and train your new pet the rules of your home.

Remember all animals are different. Some take longer to be toilet trained and adjust to a new master. Our pets need to learn to trust the people taking care of them. Be patient, be kind and let your pet know you care for him or her and you will have a good friend.

Love and kindness is the answer to having a dog like Monty.

This book has been written in honor of the pets that have passed away but have not been forgotten and are still loved by the ones that took care of them.

In Memory

I have added pets names that belonged to my family members that have gone to Heaven to live. If you would like to add your pets name to the list just write his/her name on the blank lines below.

Monty	Princess	Rufus	Alby
Molly (2)	Gurt	Skippy	Zena
Jack	Dido	Girlie	Zorro
Waldo	Penny	Lady	Beauty
Casha	_____	_____	_____
_____	_____	_____	_____

Monty

1993-2008

We know Monty is in Heaven because the Bible tells us
that God created all living things.

Special Mention

A special thank you goes out to my grandson Samuel, for keeping Monty's memory alive in his heart and for telling his sister Becca true stories about the dog he loved here on Earth. Samuel taught Becca that love can go on living in your heart even after your pet has passed away.

Samuel's eternal love for Monty has given me the inspiration to write this book.

About the Author

Barbara Norwood is a retired customer service representative for a printing company and has also worked as a quality control technician for a medical device company. She loves animals and hopes that this book will help children know it is okay to grieve openly over a pet that has passed away by sharing Monty's life story and the heartfelt testimony from Monty's family.

Printed in the United States
By Bookmasters